You Deserve More

Keep Yourself Focused as you Make that Jump!

Jumping from employee to Entrepreneur takes planning and perseverance. Remind yourself of how to make your transition simple and effective with your poster-sized copies of the tools discussed in this book. Stay focused!

Visit www.NoBossGuide.com today!

Visioning Activity	(8.5X14 in.)	$8.99
	(23X35 in.)	$24.99
NoBossGuide Pathfinder®	(8.5X14 in.)	$12.99
	(23X35 in.)	$29.99
"Take Action" Action Plan	(8.5X14 in.)	$9.99
	(23X35 in.)	$24.99

Also visit www.NoBossGuide.com for a free eCourse. Simply click on the shopping link and download "B.I.T. – There is No Box" to learn how to successfully reach your goals.

Stay focused and *Make that Jump!*

You Deserve More!

The 3 Keys to Jumping from employee to Entrepreneur

Sheron M. Brown, Ph.D.

NoBossGuide™, LLC

Laurel, Maryland

For all my friends who have dreamed of starting their own business, but were afraid.

For my uncle who always inspired me to share with the world.

For my mother who always believed.

For my son.

Dream it! Believe it! Live it!

You Deserve More! The 3 Keys to Jumping from employee to Entrepreneur
Sheron M. Brown, Ph.D.
© 2007 by Sheron M. Brown. All rights reserved.
Published by NoBossGuide™ , LLC, Laurel, MD

Cover by William Flowers (iam@mojographic.com)

This book is also published in an electronic format. Some content may vary from the electronic format of this book.

ISBN 978-0-6151-8715-0

$19.95

NoBossGuide™ , LLC
324 Main Street, Suite 1294
Laurel, MD 20707

Acknowledgements

I want to thank my partner in life and business, Brian Demps for his support and encouragement through the process of getting this book into the hands of the world. Your support kept me going whenever I slowed down. I also want to thank my good friends Patty Buffaloe and Anitra Butler. Thank you for supporting this concept and letting me know that someone in the world somewhere would benefit from what I had to share.

I am grateful for another wonderful friend and poet, David Graham. You are gifted with words and endowed with a unique ability to encourage others to move forward in their dreams. I'd also like to thank my graphic designer William Flowers for the awesome cover design and great advice. I knew I had to plan the work and work the plan. Thank you for continuing to remind me of that. Additionally, I'd like to thank my last boss I'll ever have in life. Without you, I would not have made the decision to take the leap and go confidently in the direction of my dreams. Thank you, thank you, thank you!

Finally, I want to thank God for my mind, my creativity and my courage. Because of God's universal presence and power, I am a co-creator of abundance in all things.

Table of Contents

Go confidently in the
direction of your dreams.
Live the life you've imagined.

~Thoreau

Where Are You Right Now?

If you are like many people, you wake up five, sometimes six days a week to get ready to go to a place where you don't want to go. You battle rush hour traffic, or suffer through being herded on public transportation for 30 minutes to maybe even two hours to get to your place of employment. Once there, you work long hours, only to return home tired with no time to spend with friends or family. You probably don't have time to do the things you want to do like go back to school or start your part-time business. You sit in front of your television too exhausted to do much of anything else. You complete your evening chores, put your children to bed—if you have kids—then go to bed yourself, only to wake up and begin the cycle again. You feel stuck in a rut.

Or maybe you have a different story. Maybe you actually enjoy what you do. You wake up early to walk your dog, get your children to school on time and stop at your favorite coffee shop to pick up breakfast. At your job, you work diligently to meet your deadlines and actually enjoy working with some or most of your colleagues. You then rush home at the end of the day to try to squeeze in your workout or take your children to their sports practice. Once home, you complete your evening chores, maybe do more work at home, and then begin to prepare for the next day. You may feel somewhat fulfilled, but there is still more that you want. You can't seem to find the time to do what you want and you ask yourself, "Is this what life is all about?"

No, it's not! There is more to life. There are places to visit. There are activities to enjoy with your friends and family. There are businesses to start, degrees to complete and the life that you want is waiting for you to dream it, believe it and live it! You have the right to enjoy what you do. You have the right to live a completely fulfilled life. You do not have to feel stuck in a rut. You can change the path of your life and you can begin now.

Dream it! Believe it! Live it!

3 Keys to Living the Life You Want

You can change your life today by planning. You've heard the saying, "if you fail to plan, you plan to fail." You plan your day. You make decisions about the time you must leave home to get to work on time. You plan what you will eat for dinner. You decide if you will cook, what you will cook and how you will cook it, or simply what fast food restaurant to visit. You plan a special event, whether it is a date or a party. You must also plan for the life that you want.

Dream It!

Planning for your life is simple. First you must dream it. You have to think about what you want your life to look like. Decide what you want. Do you want to start a business? Do you want to spend more time with your friends and family? Do you want to retire young and rich? Do you want to own real estate and by when do you want your dream to come true? Only you know what you want. The best way to answer this question for yourself is to ask you, "If there weren't such falsities as fear and obstacles what would be the thing(s) I'd want most?" It's okay to want to accomplish more than one major goal in life. There are many experiences to enjoy so don't feel like you have to limit yourself. Right now, stop to complete the statement below.

If there weren't such falsities as fear and obstacles, the things I'd want most are:

_____

_____

_____

_____

_____

_____

_____

Believe It!

Next, you have to believe it. You must believe that your dream is achievable and you prove this belief by your actions. You can't just dream and expect your dream to come true by sitting on your couch day after day. There is a saying that a goal without a deadline is a dream. You must make your dream a goal by setting deadlines and doing the work to make your thoughts become your reality.

By the end of this book you will outline the work that is required to making your dreams your reality. You will learn to use the NoBossGuide Pathfinder® to do the work of believing in your dreams. This tool will help you plan out your step by step actions to change your future. What you will find is that as you move toward your dream, your dream will move toward you.

Live It!

Finally, you live it. After dreaming and transforming your dream into a goal through the work of belief, you experience the ultimate. You live your dream. You have the power to create your world with your thoughts. If you believe that all there is to life is working for 30 years and retiring on your pension, then after dreaming it for 30 years and doing the work of believing it, you will live it at age sixty-something. But if you believe that you can start that business or save and invest aggressively, or enjoy your family and friends more, then you will do the work required to live that dream.

There is nothing more exhilarating than seeing your dreams becomes a reality. But there is no dream that you have that will manifest without some work behind it. You must decide that your dreams can come true. The success of your accomplishments depends on that belief.

And it's okay to be afraid, but know that fear is a result of not having a plan. You become afraid because you feel overwhelmed. And you feel overwhelmed because you don't have a plan. With a plan you are able to exhibit courage—the ability to work through the fear—because you have laid out your path. With a plan you move yourself from the unknown to the known.

After completing your NoBossGuide™ Pathfinder®, your plan will be clear and your path established. You will become empowered to dream it, believe it, live it!

Dream it! Believe it! Live it!

What is the NoBossGuide™ Pathfinder®?

The NoBossGuide Pathfinder® has its roots in a tool used in industry and government. This tool is called a Futuring Tree. The NoBossGuide Pathfinder®, like the Futuring Tree, assists with the process of creating the desired future. You begin by writing out what you want your future to look like then go through a series of activities that link your future to your present. You can liken the process to planning a road trip. When using a map, you begin the planning process by locating your destination. Next you establish your starting point. Then you do the in-between work of creating your route, or your pathway to your destination. This is the work of a NoBossGuide Pathfinder®.

Similar tools have been used for many years in industry and government to plan for business success. For example, in 1972 the managers of Shell—the oil and gas company—began the practice of futuring. They created plans to prepare for a possible change in the oil industry. By 1973 the OPEC oil embargo emerged and Shell was able to handle the changes in the industry differently and more effectively than the other large oil companies at the time. The result for Shell was success.

In 1970 Shell was labeled by Forbes as the "Ugly Sister" of the seven large oil companies, but by 1979, the company's standing in the oil industry was solid and unyielding. This was due to their planning for the future they wanted to create.

In the 1960s the National Aeronautics and Space Administration (NASA) used a tool similar to the NoBossGuide Pathfinder®, to develop the Apollo Project. Every detail was planned. NASA collected data about the moon - its measurements, and land rotations to name a few. NASA calculated how Apollo would ascend and descend along with the best locations. They also considered the earth's and moon's orbiting patterns. They identified the desired future, then carefully mapped out the details required to get them from the present to the future.

NASA (and President John F. Kennedy) dreamed of landing the first American on the moon. They believed it through their work. They lived it through the actualization of the dream. In 1969 Apollo landed safely as Neil Armstrong became the first U.S. astronaut to walk on the moon.

In both cases the unknown was planned for and became known. Imagine how scary it must have been to plan to send a man to the moon. "How do you build the ship? How will we get him up there safely? How will we get him back down to earth?" These plus hundreds of other questions must have gone through the minds of the engineers. But they planned. They created a roadmap to make the unknown known – to transform the dream into a reality.

How Can the NoBossGuide™ Pathfinder® Work for You?

So what does all this talk of industry and government planning have to do with changing your future today? Plenty! There is much talk these days about creating the reality you want through your thoughts. And while it is true that everything around us begins with a thought, it is equally true that the thought did not become someone's reality without some form of work.

In his book Maximizing Misfortune, Jerome Edmondson said, "Between vision and reality is four-letter word called WORK!" You must prepare yourself for the life you want by doing the work that will change your present reality to your desired future.

Now when you read the word *work* don't think of back-breaking process. This work is exciting because it's about you getting the life you deserve. This is the work that we live for-going after our dreams. And you can be strategic about this endeavor through using the NoBossGuide Pathfinder®.

Until now, futuring tools have mainly been used for large corporations and government planning. But the tools are equally effective for use by individuals. The NoBossGuide Pathfinder® offers you several advantages. It will help you:

1. Initiate or refine your life's vision

2. Map out the activities required to achieve your goals

3. Create the pathways that connect your present to your future

4. Plan for crucial decision making checkpoints

5. Recognize perceived barriers that can hinder your achievement

6. Analyze the most efficient ways to achieve your goals

7. Reveal the relationships between the events that create your reality

In short, the NoBossGuide Pathfinder® will lead to your life's fulfillment as you dream it—activate your thoughts; believe it—act out your faith through your works; and live it—actualize your dreams.

Strategically Create Your Desired Future

The process for developing your NoBossGuide Pathfinder® follows nine easy steps. The steps are:

1. Identify or refine your life's vision statement — this is your desired state

2. Identify your key supporters who will contribute to actualizing your vision

3. Identify the key ideas from your vision that you want actualized

4. Identify your current state — this is your present reality

5. Identify your route for your road trip from your current to desired state

6. Identify how to actualize the key vision ideas

7. Identify your path to your vision

8. Identify the most efficient route to actualizing your vision

9. Identify your action plan

That's it! The simple steps listed above are all it takes to realize your dream life — the life you deserve. But take note before we begin. Your planning may take one hour. It can take one day, a few days, or a few weeks. The timing is up to you, but you must decide now to set aside time to plan. Your current reality belongs to you. You're not pleased with it. That's why you bought this book. But there is great news. Your desired reality also belongs to you, and you can begin to make that transition today, by following the process that lies ahead.

So what are you going to do? If you want your life to stay exactly the way it is, put this book down now. Or better still; give it to someone who wants to live a more fulfilling life. But if you are that someone desiring the change, continue reading and decide right now that you will do the work required to change your current state to your desired state. Decide right now that you will dream, believe, and live the life you want…and you will do it now!

Step 1: Identify Your Life's Vision

The first thing you must be aware of is the life that you want. Do you want to make a certain amount of money? Do you want to change careers? Do you want to complete a degree in a certain amount of time? Do you want to start a business? Only you know the true answers to these questions, and so you must be honest with yourself in answering them.

When writing your vision statement you should do so in the present tense as if your future is occurring now. Do not write in an "I will" voice, but instead write with an "I am" tone. Your vision statement should draw the mental picture of how you see the life you want to have. You may be afraid to think big, but remember that to create the life you want you work with courage, that is, you work despite the fear.

We fear because of the unknown. But you are now unveiling the unknown to make it known. So really, there is nothing to fear. If you dream little, you achieve little. If you dream big you achieve big. It really is that simple. Also, your vision must evoke emotion. In doing so, your vision will inspire you to look beyond the false perceptions of fear and obstacles and help you focus on your life that waits ahead.

On the following page, I'll give you a fun and thoughtful activity to help you develop your vision for your life. If you already have one, this activity is also great for helping you to refine your desired state. The goal here is to write the vision.

The visioning activity that follows will require that you take some time to really think about what you want to know, see, say, do have, feel, believe and where you'd like to go. It's an exercise in dreaming—the first step to creating the life that you want. So settle back, turn off the T.V., get a cup of tea, if you will, and begin to dream.

Please note that at the end of the book there are samples of the activities that follow. You may want to review the samples before proceeding. You can also visit the www.nobossguide.com storee to sign up for the Dream It! eCourse.The course is designed to coach you through successfully crafting your life's vision.

Dream It: Activate Your Thoughts

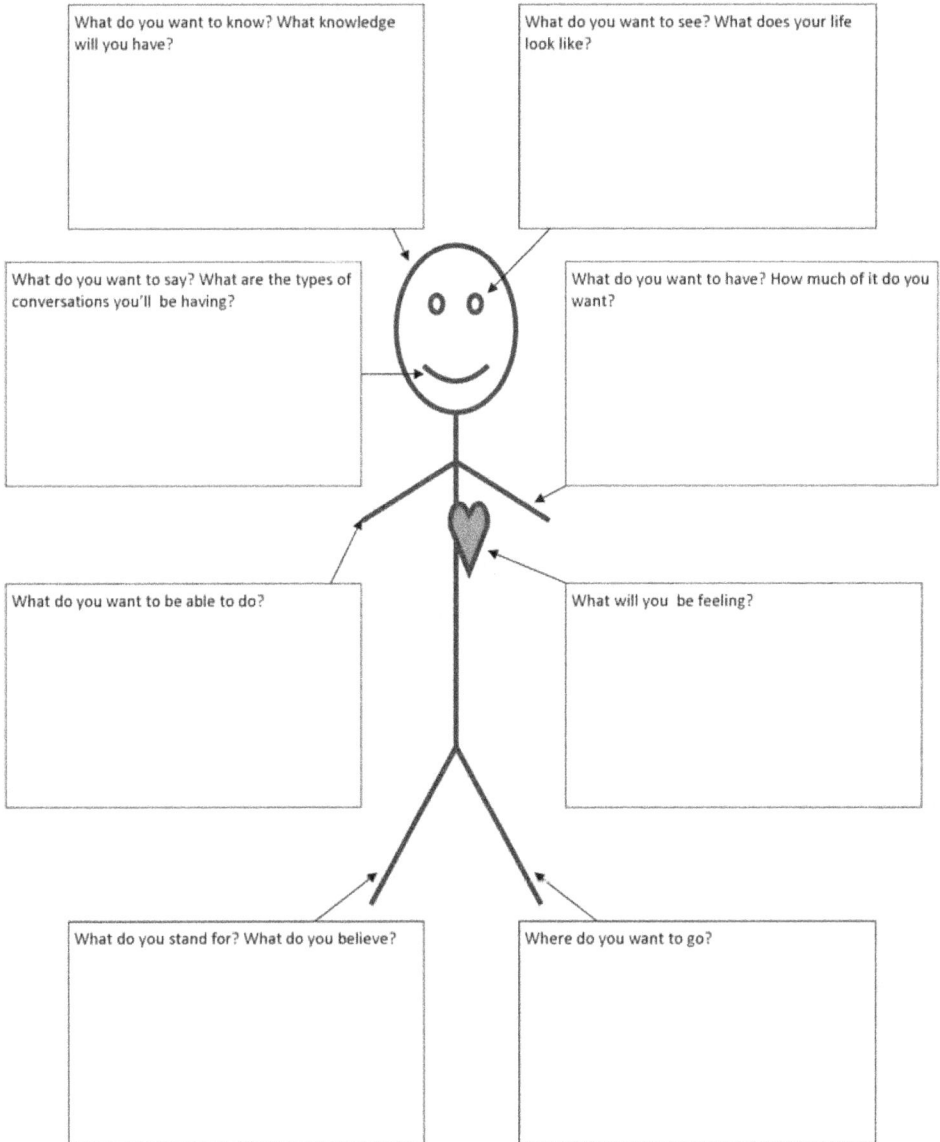

What do you want to know? What knowledge will you have?

What do you want to see? What does your life look like?

What do you want to say? What are the types of conversations you'll be having?

What do you want to have? How much of it do you want?

What do you want to be able to do?

What will you be feeling?

What do you stand for? What do you believe?

Where do you want to go?

Now that you have completed the activity, put all of your thoughts together to write your vision statement. It is okay for you to take a few hours or days to modify your vision until you are comfortable with it. You can review the vision statement at the end of the book for help with writing your own.

_____

_____

_____

_____

_____

_____

_____

_____

_____

_____

_____

_____

_____

_____

Step 2: Identify Your Key Supporters

Before going any further, you must identify the people in your life who can help you achieve your dreams. It may be your husband or your significant other. It can be your best friend or maybe even your employer, depending on what you are dreaming to create. At this point, take the time to review your vision and identify the people who will play a role in helping you achieve your dream.

You may have more or less than 10 people. Do not restrict yourself to the lines below. This is your vision, so feel free to add lines to the bottom of the page. Or you can be free to not fill in all of the lines below.

My key supporters are...

1. _____

2. _____

3. _____

4. _____

5. _____

6. _____

7. _____

8. _____

9. _____

10. _____

Step 3: Identify Key Vision Ideas

At this stage you begin the work of analyzing your vision statement to identify the key ideas. Ideally, you should create a list of two to four key ideas and the ideas should be short and to the point. Remember that you are extracting them from your vision statement.

These key ideas are important because they serve as guides as you analyze the specific steps you must take to actualize your dreams. Again, the sample section in the back of the book provides an example of key vision ideas that were extracted from the sample vision statement.

My key vision ideas are...

1. _____

2. _____

3. _____

4. _____

Step 4: Identify Your Current State

In step four you write out your current reality. It is important that you are honest with yourself when describing your current reality. If you don't have any money saved, or your credit score is below 500, then write it. You must do this to remind yourself of what you are moving away from. It is also encouraging as you move closer to your desired state to see where you came from.

Don't harp on what you do not like about your current state though. Do not allow your current state to bring you down. Remember, you are completing this exercise to map your journey from your current state to your desired state. You are empowering yourself to create the life you want. So instead of feeling badly about your current state, become excited about where you will be. Your desired future will be your current reality before you know it.

Today on _____, the _____ day of _____,

20_____ the description of my life is the following:

_____
_____
_____
_____
_____
_____
_____
_____
_____
_____
_____
_____

Step 5: Identify Your Route

This step involves you acting as a detective by searching for clues that will help you map out your route to your future. I call this *life mapping.* In mapping your route, you must work backwards to identify the actions that are required to connect your current state to your desired future. You accomplish this by answering the question, "What decision or action must occur directly before the desired future?" Once you answer this question, you ask the question again for the answer. Once you answer that question, you ask the question again.

So for example, let's say a portion of the desired state is *I live in a beautiful home by the lake.* (This example is in the sample activity portion of the book). The action that must occur exactly before becoming a homeowner is *I have to sign the paperwork at the closing table.* Then upon asking the question again, the next answer would be *I have to put a contract on a house and submit the required paperwork.* Before that, the answer would be *I have to get pre-qualified,* and before that would be *I have to improve my credit score by writing letters to the credit agencies.*

This process continues on until the root answer is found in your current reality. The root answer is a response that is embedded in your current state. For instance, in this case the current reality may state, "I have a poor credit score of 450." This would be the root and here is where you would stop asking the question. You have completed the process of connecting the activities needed between your current and desired states. This step is important because it makes you think out what actions you must take to create the life your want.

Once you have completed this process, you move on to the next step that allows you to connect your future state and key vision ideas to your present state.

Step 6: Identify How to Actualize

The next step is to create your NoBossGuide Pathfinder®. Believe it. In order to get to your destination, you must know in what direction you are to travel. Step 6 is where you determine your direction. To do this, you must analyze your key vision ideas, but you do so one at a time. This is the stage where you create your NoBossGuide Pathfinder® by analyzing your key vision ideas through six phases. Step 5 made you think. Step 6 makes you do.

To begin, you must answer a series of 6 PQ's (Pathfinder Questions). Answering these questions will help you plan for the unknown. Below, I have listed the questions and their purpose for you to have a better understanding of what you are doing and why you are doing it.

Pathfinder Question 1: What changes are needed to bring about my desired future?

This question helps you to spell out your goals. In making the list you may find that you have anywhere from two to an infinite number of answers to the question. Brainstorm and list them all. After that, you begin the work choosing one or two most pertinent to your key vision idea.

Pathfinder Question 2: What specific changes are required to establish your PQ1 goals?

This question helps you to spell out your objectives. These answers help to break down your goals even further. Again, during your brainstorming you may generate many answers, but you will have to analyze them to figure out one or two that are most important. Remember that you do this for each goal you decided on focusing on in Pathfinder Question 1.

Pathfinder Question 3: What specific strategies will help you accomplish your PQ2 objectives?

This question focuses on how you will accomplish your objectives listed in Pathfinder Question 2. You will brainstorm strategies, and choose one to two strategies that are most pertinent to accomplishing your objectives.

Pathfinder Question 4: What activities will allow your strategies in PQ3 to occur?

This question helps you to identify what activities are required in order to allow your PQ3 strategies to work. You will possibly have to make a lifestyle change.

Pathfinder Question5: What information will help you accomplish PQ1 through PQ4?

This question helps you to prepare for the change process that is ahead of you. Maybe you may need to take a course or interview experts. Please know that you are backwards planning. PQ5 is the preparation required for the questions before.

Pathfinder Question 6: What key people are needed to support the required changes?

The purpose of this question is clear. You must identify whose help you need in this change process. You may need the help of your spouse, friend or employer. Take the time to think through who can and is willing to help you. Refer to your list in Step 2 where you considered your key supporters

Notice that all the previous steps have prepared you to create your NoBossGuide Pathfinder®. Completing the Pathfinder is what helps you to believe your dream is possible. It also aids you with preparing for the unknown.

The next few pages include 4 sets of PQ's. Each set is for one key idea from your vision statement. Brainstorm each Pathfinder Question and select two of the most pertinent answers for each question. You can also visit the www.NoBossGuide store to sign up for the Believe It! eCourse. The course is designed to guide you through the process to successfully complete your NoBossGuide™ Pathfinder®.

Now, look at your first key vision idea and answer the following PQ's.

Pathfinder Questions for Key Vision Idea 1

PQ 1: What changes are needed to bring about my desired state?

_____

_____

_____

_____

_____

PQ2: What specific changes are required to establish my PQ1 goals?

_____

_____

_____

_____

PQ3: What specific strategies will help me accomplish my PQ2 objectives?

_____

_____

_____

_____

PQ4: What activities will allow my strategies in PQ3 to occur?

_____

_____

_____

_____

PQ5: What information will help me accomplish PQ1 through PQ4?

_____

_____

_____

_____

_____

PQ6: What key people are needed to support the required changes?

_____

_____

_____

_____

_____

Pathfinder Questions for Key Vision Idea 2

PQ 1: What changes are needed to bring about my desired state?

_____
_____
_____
_____
_____

PQ2: What specific changes are required to establish my PQ1 goals?

_____
_____
_____
_____

PQ3: What specific strategies will help me accomplish my PQ2 objectives?

_____
_____
_____
_____

PQ4: What activities will allow my strategies in PQ3 to occur?

_____
_____
_____
_____

PQ5: What information will help me accomplish PQ1 through PQ4?

_____

_____

_____

_____

_____

PQ6: What key people are needed to support the required changes?

_____

_____

_____

_____

_____

Pathfinder Questions for Key Vision Idea 3

PQ 1: What changes are needed to bring about my desired state?

_____
_____
_____
_____
_____

PQ2: What specific changes are required to establish my PQ1 goals?

_____
_____
_____
_____

PQ3: What specific strategies will help me accomplish my PQ2 objectives?

_____
_____
_____
_____

PQ4: What activities will allow my strategies in PQ3 to occur?

_____
_____
_____
_____

PQ5: What information will help me accomplish PQ1 through PQ4?

_____

_____

_____

_____

_____

PQ6: What key people are needed to support the required changes?

_____

_____

_____

_____

Pathfinder Questions for Key Vision Idea 4

PQ 1: What changes are needed to bring about my desired state?

_____
_____
_____
_____
_____

PQ2: What specific changes are required to establish my PQ1 goals?

_____
_____
_____
_____

PQ3: What specific strategies will help me accomplish my PQ2 objectives?

_____
_____
_____
_____

PQ4: What activities will allow my strategies in PQ3 to occur?

_____
_____
_____
_____

PQ5: What information will help me accomplish PQ1 through PQ4?

_____

_____

_____

_____

_____

PQ6: What key people are needed to support the required changes?

_____

_____

_____

_____

_____

Step 7: Identify Your Path

Believe It: Act out Your Faith through Work

Now the excitement begins! In Step 7 you create the paths that links your current to your desired state. You do this by using your responses in Step 6 to complete your NoBossGuide Pathfinder® worksheet. You begin by filling in the first column with your key vision ideas. There are four spaces, one for each key idea. You can have 1 or 3, but remember not to have more than 4. You don't want to overwhelm yourself.

Fill in your responses to PQ1 based on their relationship to the key vision idea. These are your goals. Move to the right and complete the column for PQ2 in relation to PQ1. These are your objectives. Continue this process until the worksheet has been completed. PQ3 are your strategies to meet your objectives. PQ4 address the activities you must take on in this change process. For PQ5 you must identify the information you need to make change. And in PQ6 you identify your key supporters.

As you begin to link the relationships between your responses, you will see your path reveal itself. Now read your NoBossGuide Pathfinder® from right to left and you will see that you have found your path from your current state to your desired future. You have identified the work necessary to create the life you want and deserve. You have made the unknown known. The path has been found. Believe it!

The Sample section at the end of the book gives an example of how to effectively use the NoBossGuide Pathfinder® worksheet. There is a blank Pathfinder worksheet on the following page. Use it as a guide to create your path once you have finished brainstorming your answers to PQ1 through PQ6.

NoBossGuide.com also sells poster-sized copies of the NoBossGuide Pathfinder®. The larger copies can be completed and posted in a location that has meaning for you. It can be your home office, or your workspace. Keeping your path constantly in front of you will remind you of the work that you must do to change your current state. It will also remind you that you can recreate your world. You can live your dream.

NoBossGuide™ Pathfinder®

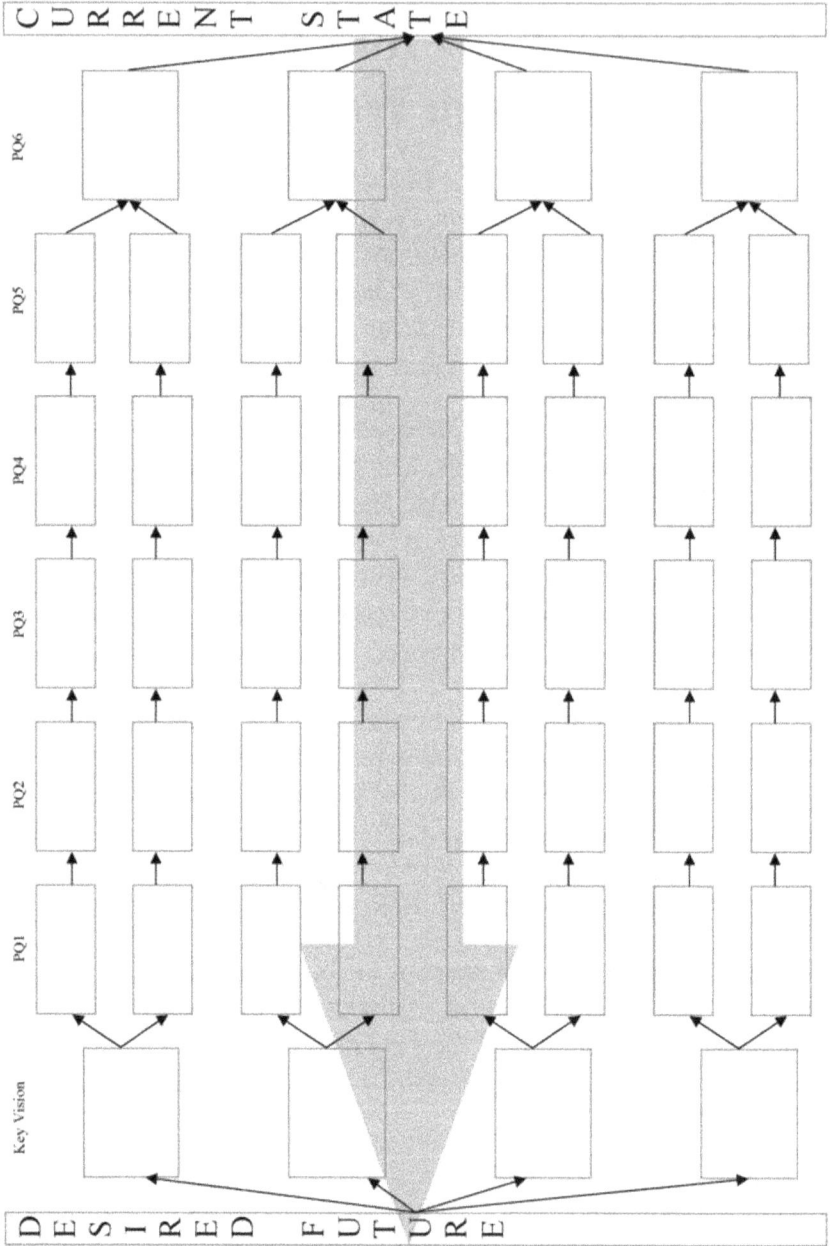

Step 8: Identify Efficiency

Congratulations! You have done great work up to this point. So far you have identified your life's vision, analyzed your current state in relation to your desired future and mapped out the route to your new life. You could stop here if you wanted to, but don't! Now is the time to perfect the work.

In Step 8 analyze your NoBossGuide Pathfinder® by reading it from right to left. Look directly to the left of to PQ6. Those are the people that are you supporters to actualizing your dreams. You want to ensure that you have listed the appropriate people. Maybe there is someone you've forgotten or someone that doesn't need to be on that list.

Once you are satisfied, look to the left again to PQ5. Make sure you have identified all the information that is required to have the knowledge to move to your desired future. If you have forgotten to add some information, then add it. If some information is redundant, then remove it.

Continue this process until you reach your key vision ideas. Ensure for yourself that you have selected the most efficient actions. When you reach the key vision idea, you must ask yourself a big question: which key idea along with its pathway can be sacrificed but still allow me to reach my desired future? This is where efficiency comes in because you are figuring out the quickest route to your desired state by eliminating the unnecessary path.

It is a challenge to eliminate a pathway, but remember this is to ensure for yourself that you have selected the most efficient actions. You don't have to eliminate a pathway, but remember this is about efficiency. If you find it is possible to do away with a pathway and still reach your desired future, then do it. You don't need any unnecessary actions slowing you down.

Step 9: Identify Your Action Plan

There is a saying, "A goal without a deadline is a dream." You began this process by dreaming—activating your thoughts. Dreaming is important. It's the activity that helps you visualize what you want. While the activity is important to the process, it doesn't end there. For this to work, you must make a commitment to yourself by adding dates to your activities. You can accomplish this by using your NoBossGuide Pathfinder® to create an action plan.

The following page has a blank action plan for your use. A poster-sized copy of the plan can be purchased through NoBossGuide.com. An important note: do not beat up on yourself if you set a date and are forced to change the date. Remember, in some cases you will be relying on others for a favor and you cannot control them. But you can remind and encourage them or sometimes you can figure out how to accomplish the task without their help—especially if their procrastination is slowing you down beyond reason. Do not use their procrastination as an excuse to delay for months or years. A 2-3 week setback is fine, but get on it. Do the work!

The NoBossGuice™ website offers the Live It! eCourse that guides you through the process of completing the Take Action action plan. Visit www.NoBossGuide.com to learn more about this offering.

Take Action Plan

Required Action	Key Person for Support	Completion Date	Required Resources	Places to Contact	How to Accomplish	Benchmark of Accomplishment
1.						
2.						
3.						
4.						
5.						
6.						
7.						
8.						
9.						
10.						
11.						
12						

Live it: Actualize Your Dreams

There you have. Nine simple steps to creating the life you want and deserve. You can have it if you choose it. But you must choose. You do not have to live someone else's life. You do not have to live the life that others have chosen for you. You do not have to live the life that your paycheck dictates. You can do something about it.

Invest time in yourself. You must decide that you will take the time to complete your NoBossGuide.com Pathfinder®. Commit to 30 minutes a day to begin the work of changing your life. Thirty minutes every day equals 3.5 hours per week. Three and a half hours per week is approximately 14 hours per month and 112 hours per year. One hundred and twelve hours a year is 4 ½ days—4 ½ days to change your life! That's all it takes to begin the change process that will lead you to the life you want. It is highly possible that you can complete the process in a week or less, but the point here is that it doesn't take much to change your life if you commit to investing time in yourself.

Don't give up. Have you ever heard that fear is "false expectations appearing real?" You must decide that despite what you've been told about yourself, despite the doubts, despite what things may look like, if you are diligent and focused, you will actualize your dream for your life.

Be grateful. Show your gratitude to your key supporters as they help you actualize your dreams. Let them know that you are grateful for their support and presence in your life. Also, take the time to enjoy life. When you work, be steadfast, but don't forget to play. Balancing your life is a priority for yourself and your family.

Remember, invest in yourself, be diligent about planning the work and working the plan and always be grateful for those who are in your life. Iß guarantee that you'll:

Dream It! Activate your thoughts

Believe It! Act out your faith through work

Live It! Actualize your dreams

Leap!
And the net will appear.

~Zen Saying

Samples

This section is a guide to using the tools outlined in this book. You can use it to better understand what you read, or to generate ideas for yourself. The next few pages that follow show the samples of the following tools.

1. Sample Visioning Activity

2. Sample Vision Statement (Desired State)

3. Sample List of Key Supporters

4. Sample Key Vision Ideas

5. Sample Current State

6. Sample NoBossGuide™ Pathfinder®

Also remember to visit www.NoBossGuide.com for continued guidance on making your dream real.

Sample Visioning Activity

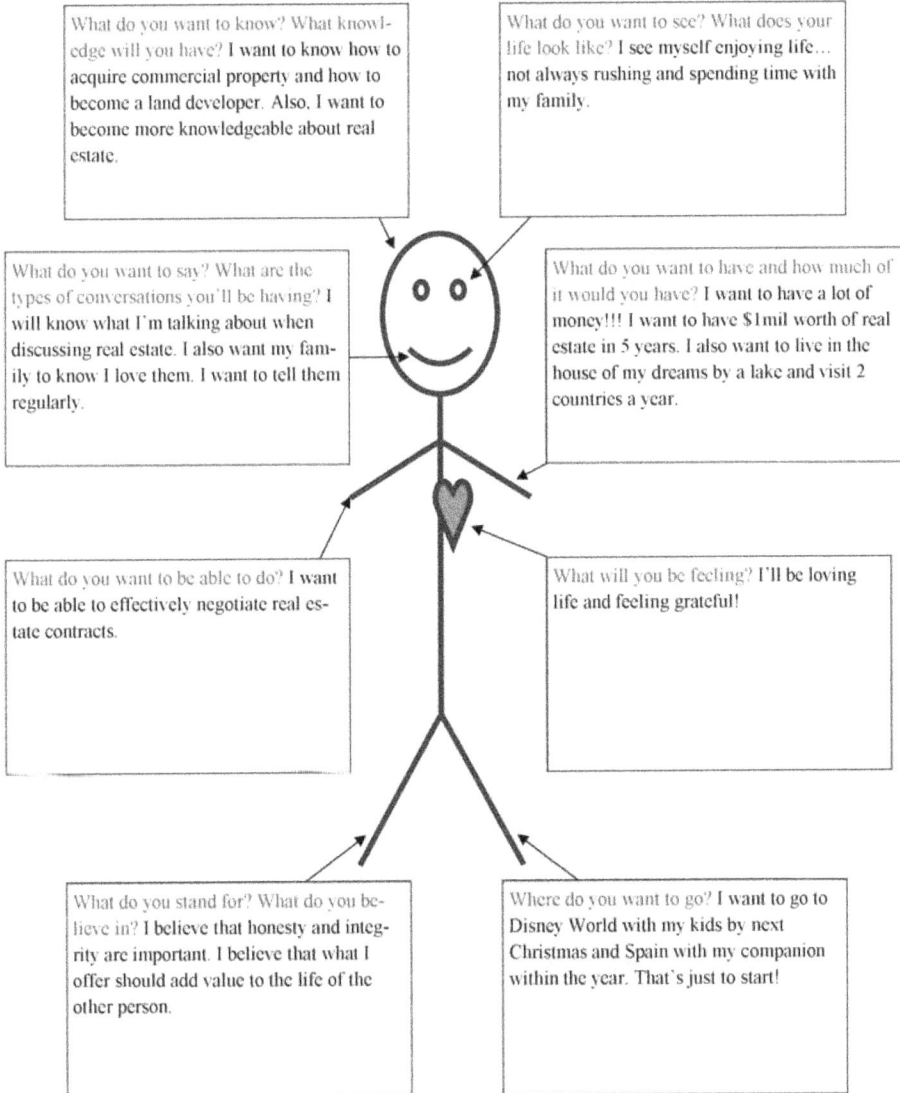

What do you want to know? What knowledge will you have? I want to know how to acquire commercial property and how to become a land developer. Also, I want to become more knowledgeable about real estate.

What do you want to see? What does your life look like? I see myself enjoying life... not always rushing and spending time with my family.

What do you want to say? What are the types of conversations you'll be having? I will know what I'm talking about when discussing real estate. I also want my family to know I love them. I want to tell them regularly.

What do you want to have and how much of it would you have? I want to have a lot of money!!! I want to have $1mil worth of real estate in 5 years. I also want to live in the house of my dreams by a lake and visit 2 countries a year.

What do you want to be able to do? I want to be able to effectively negotiate real estate contracts.

What will you be feeling? I'll be loving life and feeling grateful!

What do you stand for? What do you believe in? I believe that honesty and integrity are important. I believe that what I offer should add value to the life of the other person.

Where do you want to go? I want to go to Disney World with my kids by next Christmas and Spain with my companion within the year. That's just to start!

Sample Vision Statement – Desired Future

I enjoy my life because I spend plenty of time with my family. I travel the world regularly and live in a beautiful home by the lake. I also travel regularly to other countries. I own commercial property worth $1,000,000.00 and when I broker my deals, I do so with honesty and integrity. This is my life and I have joy!

Sample Key Supporters

1. My companion
2. My mother and companion's mother
3. My friend the real estate agent
4. My cousin the attorney
5. My neighbor the accountant

Sample Key Vision Ideas

1. Purchase dream home by the lake
2. Acquire commercial property worth $1mil
3. Increase travel

Sample Current State

I only see my children for about three hours per week evening. I rush home from work to pick them up from after-care at 6 P.M., hurry to make dinner and possibly check homework, and then get them to bed by 9 P.M. On the weekends they have sports practice so I'm driving all day doing that and running errands. I see my companion about twice a week. He has two jobs, and so it seems like he's either always working or tired or both! We haven't taken a vacation in eight years. I live in an apartment where we don't feel safe. At this moment, I am unfamiliar with how the real estate game works and my credit score is only 450.

Sample Route: Key Vision Idea 2

Acquire Commercial Property worth $1mil

Pathfinder Question 1: What changes are needed in bring about my desired future?

I want to be a real estate broker with focused knowledge in commercial property and land development.

Pathfinder Question 2: What specific changes are required to establish my PQ1 goals?

I need to move from not knowing to knowing. I must take a class in real estate either at the community college or through a broker. I also have to establish myself as an appropriate business structure.

Pathfinder Question 3: What specific strategies will accomplish PQ2 objectives?

Compare the cost of classes along with the dates and times they are offered. I also have to gather information on different business structures.

Pathfinder Question 4: What activities will allow my strategies in PQ3 to occur?

I have to talk to my companion and our mothers to see how we can work out the time for me to take these classes. If the classes are on the weekend then someone needs to take the kids to their games. I need to research the business structures and consult with an attorney.

Pathfinder Question5: What information will help me accomplish PQ1 through PQ4?

I need to know the logistics of the classes as far as the days and times. I need to schedule time to talk to an attorney.

Pathfinder Question 6: What key people are needed to support the required changes?

My companion and our mothers are the key supporters for this dream. My cousin the tax attorney is also a supporter.

Dream it! Believe it! Live it!

Sample NoBossGuide™ Pathfinder®

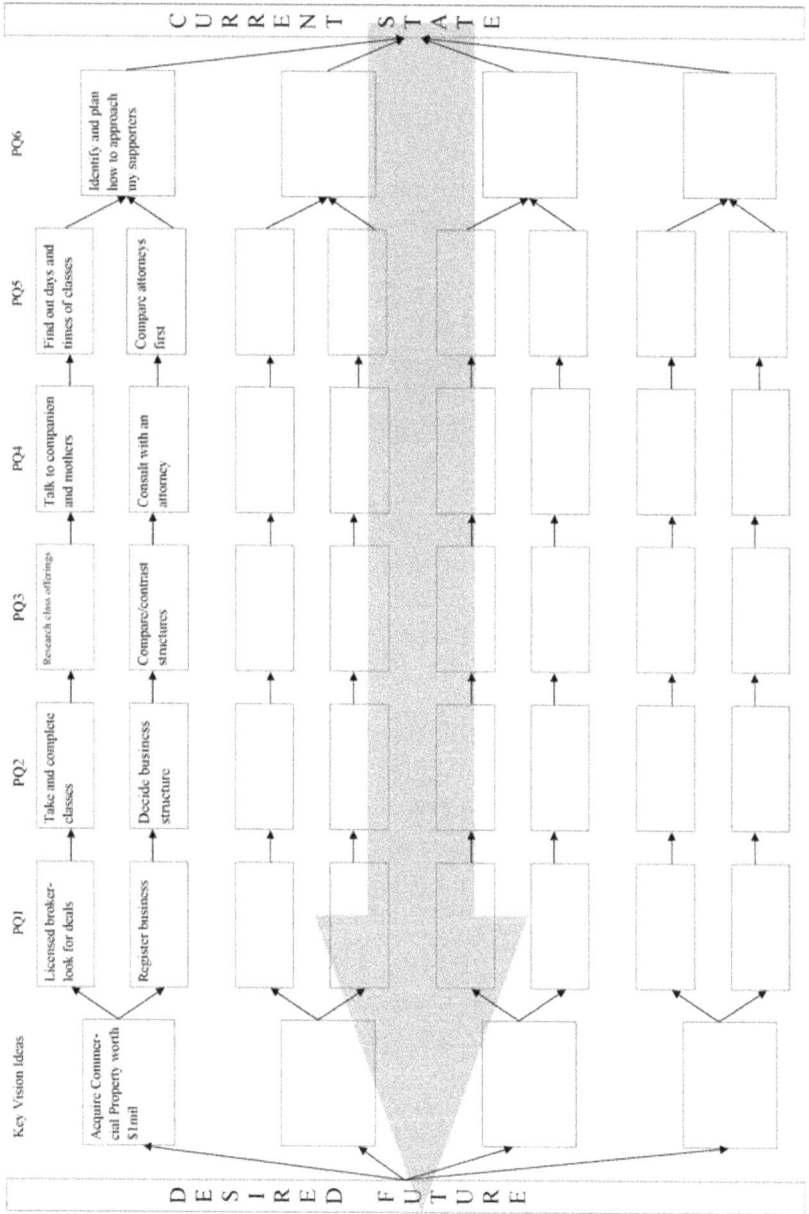

Page 56

Keep Yourself Focused as you Make that Jump!

Jumping from employee to Entrepreneur takes planning and perseverance. Remind yourself of how to make your transition simple and effective with your poster-sized copies of the tools discussed in this book. Stay focused!

Visit www.NoBossGuide.com today!

Visioning Activity	(8.5X14 in.)	$8.99
	(23X35 in.)	$24.99
NoBossGuide Pathfinder®	(8.5X14 in.)	$12.99
	(23X35 in.)	$29.99
"Take Action" Action Plan	(8.5X14 in.)	$9.99
	(23X35 in.)	$24.99

Also visit www.NoBossGuide.com for a free eCourse. Simply click on the shopping link and download "B.I.T. – There is No Box" to learn how to successfully reach your goals.

Stay focused and *Make that Jump!*

Notes

Dream It! Believe It! Live It!

About the Author

Photo by Jim Buckley

Dr. Sheron Brown is a Change Strategist who coaches individuals on transitioning from their role of employee to entrepreneur. Dr. Brown offers a wide range of programs and services – from individual change management tools to eCourses in personal goal design and personalized transition coaching.

After a successful 10-year career in facilitating change through employee development training, Dr. Brown now coaches individuals for success in personal and professional transitioning.

To contact her, please email DrFreedom@NoBossGuide.com.

www.ingramcontent.com/pod-product-compliance
Lightning Source LLC
Chambersburg PA
CBHW021349090426
42742CB00008B/794

9 7 8 0 6 1 5 1 8 7 1 5 0